HENRY VIII

BY

JOHN GUY

THE YOUNG HENRY

Henry came to the throne at the age of 17, a handsome, strong, giant of a man. He stood 1.83 metres (6ft) tall at a time when the average height was just 1.6 metres (5.2ft). He was not prepared for becoming king and did not know how to rule the country. A larger-than-life character, Henry wasted his father's fortune and was more interested in sports, music and dancing than in politics. He left important decisions to a group of trusted ministers.

CEREMONIAL ARMOUR

This suit of armour, with silver and fine engraving, was made for Henry. It was used for parading during tournaments.

THE THRILL OF THE HUNT

Henry loved to hunt in the forests attached to the royal palaces, particularly with birds of prey. Hunting had many rules. Kestrels, such as this, were flown by less important nobles and by Henry when he was learning the sport. Later, he would probably have flown a larger bird, such as the peregrine falcon or an eagle.

HENRY VIII

This portrait miniature shows Prince Henry as a young boy. He was the third child (and second son) of Henry VII. He was not born to rule and only came to the throne because of his brother Arthur's early death in 1502.

HENRY VII

Henry VII was born at Pembroke Castle in 1457. He was an only child and became the last surviving male heir of the Lancastrians aged 14. For his own safety Henry was sent to France during the War of the Roses, where he remained for 14 years.

KEY EVENTS OF HENRY'S LIFE

-1485-
Battle of Bosworth Field. War of the Roses ends. Henry VII crowned king.

-1486-
Prince Arthur born.

-1491-
Prince Henry (later Henry VIII) born.

-1502-
Prince Arthur dies.

-1509-
Henry VII dies. Prince Henry becomes king. His coronation takes place at Westminster Abbey on 24 June.

THE TUDORS COME TO POWER

Henry VII defeated King Richard III at the battle of Bosworth Field on 22 August 1485 and Henry was crowned king of England at the age of 28, beginning the reign of the Tudors. This ended the War of the Roses, which had been going on between the House of York (Richard) and the House of Lancaster (Henry) for 30 years.

THE GOLDEN YEARS

When he came to the throne as a strong, charming teenager, Henry was welcomed. The people rejoiced as the years of harsh control under Henry VII ended. The 'Golden Years' of Henry's reign coincided with his first marriage to Catherine of Aragon. Henry VIII appeared to promise much, but he did not live up to expectations and his behaviour became more extreme with each of his five marriages.

THE KING'S DEPARTURE

The scene at Dover, May 1520, when Henry and his court of 5,800 set off for their meeting with King Francis I of France, to improve European relations (later known as 'Field of the Cloth of Gold', see p21).

THE 'UNKNOWN' WARRIOR

Henry was very good at jousting. He sometimes fought as an unknown contestant, only to later reveal his true identity as the victor to the cheering crowds, who no doubt pretended to be fooled!

PUNISHMENT FROM GOD?

Catherine was not able to give Henry a son and heir. Henry believed this was God's punishment for marrying his brother's widow. He tried to have the marriage annulled so he could marry someone else.

4

COUNTRY RETREAT

The Tudor banqueting hall of Leeds Castle, Kent. Henry built a fine suite of royal apartments here for use when he wished to escape London.

~1513~
Scottish defeated in the Battle of Flodden Field in Northumberland.

French defeated in the Battle of the Spurs.

~1520~
Henry's meeting with Francis I of France ('Field of the Cloth of Gold').

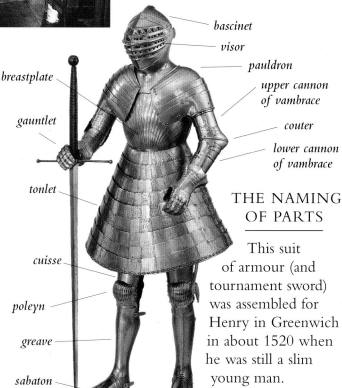

- bascinet
- visor
- pauldron
- upper cannon of vambrace
- breastplate
- gauntlet
- couter
- lower cannon of vambrace
- tonlet
- cuisse
- poleyn
- greave
- sabaton

THE NAMING OF PARTS

This suit of armour (and tournament sword) was assembled for Henry in Greenwich in about 1520 when he was still a slim young man.

SEAL OF APPROVAL

Henry VIII's Great Seal, which was stamped onto all official royal documents, including the many death warrants issued against his enemies.

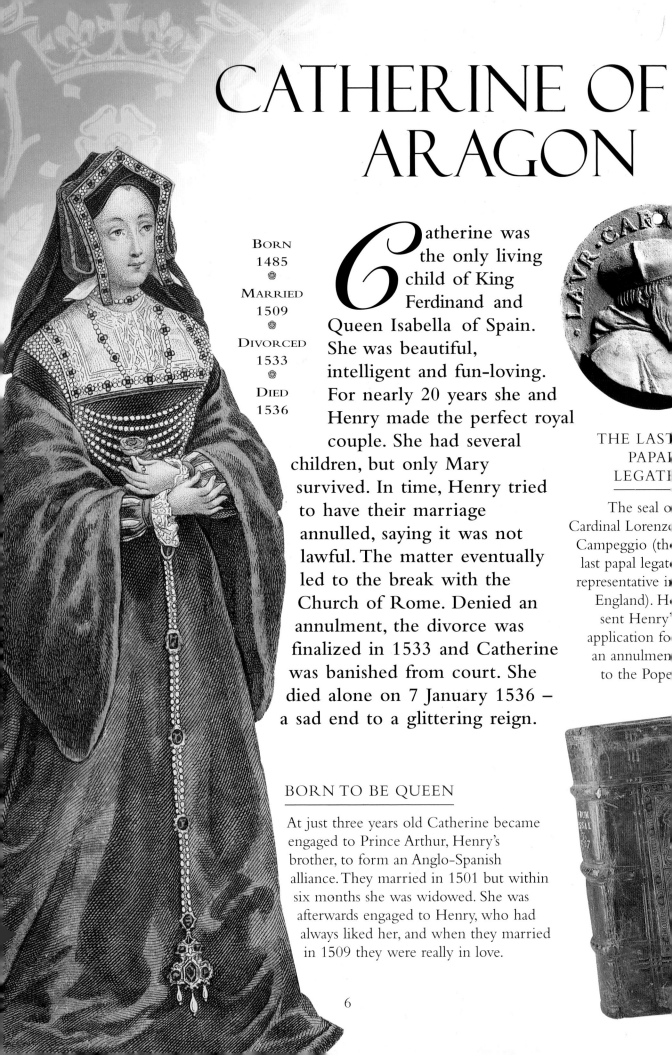

CATHERINE OF ARAGON

BORN
1485
❀
MARRIED
1509
❀
DIVORCED
1533
❀
DIED
1536

Catherine was the only living child of King Ferdinand and Queen Isabella of Spain. She was beautiful, intelligent and fun-loving. For nearly 20 years she and Henry made the perfect royal couple. She had several children, but only Mary survived. In time, Henry tried to have their marriage annulled, saying it was not lawful. The matter eventually led to the break with the Church of Rome. Denied an annulment, the divorce was finalized in 1533 and Catherine was banished from court. She died alone on 7 January 1536 – a sad end to a glittering reign.

THE LAST PAPAL LEGATE

The seal of Cardinal Lorenzo Campeggio (the last papal legate representative in England). He sent Henry's application for an annulment to the Pope.

BORN TO BE QUEEN

At just three years old Catherine became engaged to Prince Arthur, Henry's brother, to form an Anglo-Spanish alliance. They married in 1501 but within six months she was widowed. She was afterwards engaged to Henry, who had always liked her, and when they married in 1509 they were really in love.

CATHERINE'S DEFENCE

After much discussion, Catherine's hearing to fight Henry's application for a divorce began on 18 June 1529. She argued to the court that she and Arthur never lived as man and wife, so her marriage to Henry was legal.

PERSONAL HYGIENE

Catherine was very particular about her own cleanliness. This very comfortable bathroom, with its fire and linen-lined tub, is very typical of those in the royal palaces.

KEY EVENTS OF HENRY'S LIFE

~1509~
Henry marries Catherine of Aragon.

~1511~
Prince Henry born to Catherine and Henry.

Infant Prince Henry dies.

~1533~
Henry 'officially' divorces Catherine of Aragon.

~1536~
Catherine of Aragon dies.

CATHERINE'S MISSAL

Catherine was very religious and had her own missal (prayer book), bound in leather, which she took to mass to follow the prayers.

PRINCESS MARY

Mary was the only child of Catherine and Henry to survive. Born on 18 February 1516 she was largely ignored by Henry after his divorce from Catherine. At that time her rights to the throne were barred by Parliament. She was later crowned Queen Mary I in 1553.

PATRON OF THE ARTS

Although usually regarded as a strong, powerful leader, and even a tyrant in the latter years of his reign, Henry also had a gentler side to his nature. He was a patron (supporter) of the arts. He liked to surround himself with beautiful objects and bought many paintings, statues and wood carvings. He furnished his many palaces beautifully and collected many pieces of jewellery and fine art, such as clocks. Hans Holbein, a German portrait painter, was employed to paint the royal family. Henry also started a new fashion at court – composing music and setting verses to it.

DEVOUTLY RELIGIOUS

Henry was a surprisingly devout Catholic until his divorce from Catherine. This illustration, from Henry's own book of psalms shows the king reading religious texts, some of which he set to music.

COURTLY MUSIC

Professional musicians were employed to entertain the king at court and accompany him on his travels. Musicians nearly always performed in private, seldom at public functions, except dances. This lute – an early form of guitar – and flute (left) are typical Tudor instruments.

A MAN OF LETTERS

Henry was a brilliant scholar, though he found writing rather tedious. He dictated most of his official letters, but wrote his private correspondence, and poetry himself. His personal writing box is shown here, decorated with the royal coat of arms. It was made of painted wood and gilt leather.

AN ACCOMPLISHED MUSICIAN

Henry himself was a talented musician and is said to have had a good singing voice. He is also thought to have written a number of songs, including possibly the words to 'Greensleeves'.

KEY EVENTS OF HENRY'S LIFE

~1497/8~
Hans Holbein the Younger is born.

~1536~
Holbein becomes Henry's court painter.

A KEEN READER

Henry was a keen reader and could speak English, Spanish, French and Latin. He encouraged reading and insisted that his children were taught to read at an early age.

PRIVATE PERFORMANCE

Women had few privileges at court, but Henry allowed any who were good musicians to give private recitals. The woman in this picture is playing an early form of fiddle.

BREAK WITH THE CHURCH OF ROME

HENRY DEFIES THE POPE

This contemporary woodcut (c.1538) shows the Pope as an antichrist, and Henry defying papal power. It is typical of the anti-Catholic feeling that swept Europe in the 16th century.

There was already a growing number of people protesting against corruption within the Catholic Church. This objection was started by Martin Luther in 1517 and quickly spread across Europe. These people came to be known as Protestants, and seized upon the opportunity to establish a new Church in England by siding with the king. When the Pope refused to annul his marriage to Catherine of Aragon, Henry decided to take away the power of the clergy by Act of Parliament. However, despite this, Henry remained a Catholic throughout his life. The conversion of the Church of England to Protestantism came later, during Elizabeth I's reign.

THE REFORMATION

In 1533 Parliament passed the Act of Appeals, asserting England's independence from Rome. The following year the Act of Supremacy made Henry 'Supreme Head of the Church of England'.

THE ARREST OF THOMAS MORE

Sir Thomas More, Lord Chancellor and chief minister at the time, was a devout Catholic and refused to acknowledge Henry as head of the English Church. He was arrested and executed in 1535.

DEFENDER OF THE FAITH

Ironically, in 1521 Henry wrote a book defending the Catholic faith against the Protestant writings of Martin Luther, earning him the title 'Defender of the Faith' from the Pope. The abbreviation F.D. (*Fidei Defensor* in Latin) still appears on coins today.

WILLIAM WARHAM

Archbishop of Canterbury from 1504 to 1532, Warham had married Henry and Catherine. He fought against Henry's break with the Church of Rome all his life.

DEFENDING THE REALM

CANNON FIRE

Detail of a bronze demi cannon, found aboard the *Mary Rose*. All of Henry's guns carried the royal design of a rose.

*H*enry VIII was an ambitious man, personally and politically. He took part in several military campaigns to strengthen his position in Europe, with varying degrees of success. Charles V – the Holy Roman Emperor – was Catherine of Aragon's nephew, and had already successfully attacked Rome, putting the Pope under his control. When Henry later asked the Pope's permission to divorce Catherine, he was not received favourably. Following Henry's split with the Church of Rome, he spent the last years of his reign under threat of an invasion to re-establish the Pope's authority. As protection, Henry built a chain of fortifications along the south coast of England.

THE ENGLISH NAVY

Although founded by his father, it was Henry VIII who first developed the navy into a proper fighting force. By the end of his reign he had a fleet of 80 ships.

LINES OF DEFENCE

Deal Castle, Kent, as it appeared when newly completed in 1540. The largest of the Henrician (meaning, 'of Henry's reign') coastal forts, it was also the most powerful, defended by cannons and handguns.

HENRY'S SOUTH COAST FORTIFICATIONS

This map shows Henry's castle-building programme to protect the south coast from attack by Spain and France. The defences were mostly built between 1538 and 1540 with money and materials from the recently closed monasteries.

St Ives •
Falmouth •
Pendennis •
St Mawes •
Plymouth Citadel •
Paignton •
Torquay •
Dartmouth •
Teignmouth •
Exmouth •
Sidmouth •

FORTRESS PALACE

The only royal palace to be heavily fortified was the Tower of London. Dating from Norman times, it was a large fortress guarding Henry's capital city.

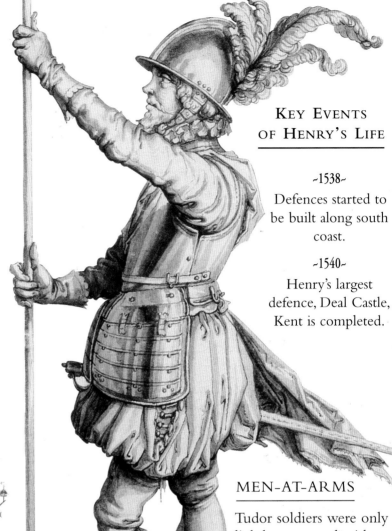

KEY EVENTS OF HENRY'S LIFE

~1538~
Defences started to be built along south coast.

~1540~
Henry's largest defence, Deal Castle, Kent is completed.

MEN-AT-ARMS

Tudor soldiers were only lightly armoured with helmets and breastplates (similar to this illustration). They were expected to provide their own weapons, which might be pistols, muskets, pikestaffs or even crossbows.

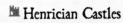

- 🏰 Henric an Castles
- 🏯 Henrician Blockhouses
- ✳ Other Forts and Castles
- ● Towns

London · Tilbury · Shoeburyness · Margate · Greenwich · Gravesend · Chatham · Sheerness · Sandwich · Sandown · Deal · Walmer · Dover · Folkestone · Sandgate · Hythe · Romney · Camber · Rye · Winchelsea · Hastings · Pevensey · Eastbourne · Beachy Head · Worthing · Brighton · Bodiam · Bognor · Chichester · Portsmouth · Southsea · Fort Nelson · Portchester · Fort Brockhurst · Cowes · Sandown · Carisbrooke · Calshot · Hurst · Yarmouth · Southampton · Bournemouth · Swanage · Brownsea · Poole · Sandsfoot · Portland

ANNE BOLEYN

BORN	1502
MARRIED	1533
DIVORCED	1536
EXECUTED	1536

*W*hen Henry realized that Catherine was not going to give him a son, he began to lose interest in her. Henry had many affairs, including one with Anne Boleyn. He fell in love with her and they married in secret probably on 25 January 1533, four months before Henry was divorced from Catherine. But Anne also failed to have a baby son and Henry decided to end their marriage. He accused Anne of having affairs and of plotting to murder him. On 17 May 1536, Henry had his marriage to Anne annulled. She was executed on 19 May.

WAITING TO DIE

On 24 April 1536 Anne's uncle, the Duke of Norfolk, was ordered by Thomas Cromwell to give evidence against her. While she was imprisoned in the Tower of London, Anne etched her name into the wall of her prison cell.

SIGN OF THE TIMES

The date of Anne's birth is not known but is usually thought to be 1502. She was not a very beautiful woman and had six fingers on one hand. Henry used this against her, saying it was a sign of witchcraft.

THE FUTURE QUEEN

Anne gave birth to Elizabeth on 7 September 1533, eight months after her 'official' marriage to Henry. Henry was disappointed that she was not a boy but she eventually became queen in 1558.

KEY EVENTS OF HENRY'S LIFE

~1533~
Henry secretly marries Anne Boleyn.

Princess Elizabeth born.

~1536~
Henry divorces Anne Boleyn.

Execution of Anne Boleyn.

ANNE'S JEWEL BOX

Anne loved her jewellery. She carried it in this box on her journeys between the royal palaces. It is on display at Leeds Castle, Kent, one of her favourite homes.

MARY BOLEYN

Anne's elder sister, Mary, had an affair with Henry in 1521. It is thought she might have had his son. Anne was made Queen Catherine's lady-in-waiting and then Henry lost interest in Mary.

CHILDHOOD HOME

Anne's family home was Hever Castle, Kent. It was built in 1340 and extended by her father, Sir Thomas Bullen (or Boleyn). Anne's ghost is said to haunt the gardens at Hever each Christmas.

EXECUTIONER'S SWORD

Anne was taken to Tower Green just before noon, wearing a black robe. A skilled executioner was brought over from France at her request. He may have used a sword similar to this one.

15

THE ROYAL PALACES

TUDOR KITCHENS

The kitchens at Hampton Court as they were in Henry's day.

Henry VIII spent a vast fortune on his royal residences, improving existing palaces and building some new ones too. He was determined to show off his wealth and power to all the leaders of Europe. Henry's household regularly visited each of the palaces at different times of the year.

HAMPTON COURT PALACE

Hampton Court began as a small medieval manor, belonging to the Knights Hospitallers – a religious order. Greatly extended by Cardinal Wolsey into a palace, he was forced to give it to Henry in 1528, who extended it still further.

NONSUCH PALACE

In 1538 Henry began his most ambitious building project, the Palace of Nonsuch, in Surrey. It was to be the most magnificent palace in Europe, but was never completed. Today, all trace of it has gone.

GREENWICH PALACE

The Tudor palace of Placentia, birthplace of Henry VIII and Elizabeth I, stood by the River Thames at Greenwich, then just a village outside London. It was a magnificent medieval palace. Although rebuilt by Charles II to designs by Sir Christopher Wren, this view by the painter Canaletto (c.1750) gives a good idea of the grandeur of the riverside setting. The buildings were later turned into a naval hospital, college and museum.

JANE SEYMOUR

BORN
1509

MARRIED
1536

DIED
1537

*W*hen Henry began to lose interest in Anne, soon after the birth of Princess Elizabeth, he turned to Jane Seymour, the queen's lady-in-waiting. However, Jane refused gold, returned Henry's letters unopened, and made him promise never to speak to her except in the company of others. The king moved Jane's brother, Edward, into the palace to act as chaperone. Henry and Jane were eventually married just two weeks after Anne Boleyn's execution. She gave birth to Edward on 12 October 1537 – the only one of Henry's sons to survive. Jane was a kind and gentle woman and helped unite Henry and his daughter Princess Mary.

UNCROWNED QUEEN

Although many consider Jane Seymour to have been Henry's favourite wife, sadly she was never actually crowned queen before her death on 24 October 1537.

THE FUTURE KING

As a young child Edward was intelligent and quite strong, but he later suffered from a number of illnesses. In January 1553 he got tuberculosis and died six months later, at just 15 years old. He was the first king to be crowned 'Supreme Head of the English Church'.

SALT OF THE EARTH

In medieval and Tudor times salt was very expensive and important because it was essential for the preservation of food. Francis I, King of France, presented this combined clock and salt cellar to Henry – a very fine gift.

BIRTH AND DEATH

Jane had a long labour with Edward, finally giving birth by Caesarean section, the surgeons using implements similar to these. Complications set in, and she died of blood poisoning two weeks later.

KEY EVENTS OF HENRY'S LIFE

~1536~
Henry marries Jane Seymour.

~1537~
Prince Edward born.

Jane Seymour dies.

THE KING MOURNS

Henry is said to have really loved Jane and was very upset when she died. Her body was laid to rest at Windsor, where Henry was later buried. She is the only wife to share his grave.

EUROPEAN RELATIONS

WRESTLING

Henry VIII loved to wrestle, but he was beaten by Francis I during a friendly match.

*W*hen Henry came to the throne, England was not an important country within Europe. Being a proud man, he was keen to succeed on the battlefield and took part in several minor campaigns, with mixed results. In 1513 he joined forces with the Emperor Maximilian against France. When Cardinal Wolsey's attempts to gain power in Europe failed, it left Henry alone, with no support. Wolsey was arrested in 1530 but died on the journey to the Tower of London.

THE FIELD OF THE CLOTH OF GOLD (1520)

After many years of war, there was a fragile peace in Europe.
Henry had managed to keep France and Spain from fighting
each other. Cardinal Wolsey organized a meeting between
Henry and Francis I of France outside Calais to try to agree a
formal alliance supporting each other. Henry put up a small
'town' of tents and pavilions to house the two kings and their
servants. He wore a gold cloak, and the meeting became
known as 'The Field of the Cloth of Gold'.

KEY EVENTS OF HENRY'S LIFE

~1520~
'Field of the Cloth
of Gold'.

~1528~
Cardinal Wolsey gives
Hampton Court
to Henry.

~1530~
Wolsey arrested,
later dies.

~1544~
Siege of Boulogne.

SIEGE OF BOULOGNE

This woodcut
shows Henry's army
laying siege to
Boulogne in 1544.
Powerful cannons
break through the
walls, while armed
knights wait to
enter the city.

THOMAS WOLSEY
(1475–1530)

Cardinal Wolsey, although
of humble birth, was made Lord
Chancellor by Henry
in 1514. He was a
powerful politician
who was in charge of
the country for 15
years, until he fell
from favour in 1529.

ANNE OF CLEVES

BORN
1515

MARRIED
1540

DIVORCED
1540

DIED
1557

*H*enry seems to have really grieved for Jane Seymour and did not remarry until two years after her death. Until then, Henry had married the women of his own choice, which was unusual because royal marriages were normally arranged. Thomas Cromwell and several other of the king's ministers were becoming increasingly worried about Henry's role in Europe, and were keen for the king to make a good marriage to strengthen his position. Charles V of Spain and Francis I of France were gathering an army against England. They wanted to re-establish papal power, and Henry desperately needed an ally in Europe. So he agreed to a political marriage, even after the threat of invasion passed.

MATCHMAKER

Thomas Cromwell, Henry's current chief minister, was given the task of finding the king a new wife. A useful political alliance between England and Germany might be formed if he could persuade Henry to marry one of the Duke of Cleves' sisters.

A COMFORTABLE RETIREMENT

Henry and Anne were a disappointment to one another from the start. She could speak no English and had few social graces. Educated more in domestic skills than in art, literature and music, all of which Henry loved, Anne retired to Richmond Palace, where she lived peacefully until her death in 1557.

IMMEDIATE DIVORCE

The marriage was not a success and Henry wanted an immediate divorce, which was granted six months later.

THE 'FLANDERS MARE'

Hans Holbein was sent to Germany to paint portraits of Anne and her sister Amelia. Henry chose Anne and agreed to marry her on the strength of it, but was later very disappointed with her, calling her the 'Flanders Mare'.

KEY EVENTS OF HENRY'S LIFE

~1539~
Hans Holbein paints Anne's portrait.

~1540~
Henry marries Anne of Cleves.

Henry divorces Anne of Cleves.

DISSOLUTION OF THE MONASTERIES

'PILGRIMS OF GRACE'

Robert Aske led a pilgrimage from Yorkshire to London to demand that Henry reopen the monasteries. It was a peaceful protest, but Henry had Aske and many of his followers executed.

*I*n Henry's time there were about 850 monasteries in England and Wales, housing about 9,000 monks and nuns. Many of their traditional duties, such as writing books and healing the sick, had been taken over by people such as doctors. Standards had fallen, but most of the criticisms of the monks and nuns were not true. As the new head of the Church, Henry saw his chance to close the monasteries down and take their money. Thomas Cromwell was responsible for 'dissolving', or closing the monasteries between 1536 and 1540.

REUSED STONE

The monasteries served as 'quarries' for stone in Henry's castle-building programme, as shown left.

A TYPICAL DAY IN A MONASTERY

Midnight	Matins (church service)
1am	Retire to bed
5am	Prime (church service)
6am	Breakfast
7am	Work duties
9am	Chapter Mass (church service)
10am	Meeting with abbot
11am	High Mass (church service)
12 noon	Dinner
1pm	Rest in dormitory
2pm	Work duties
4pm	Vespers (church service)
5pm	Work duties
6pm	Supper
7pm	Evening Prayer
8pm	Retire to bed

NO CHANCE TO REFUSE

Cromwell's officials visited each monastery and requested that the monks close it down voluntarily, forfeiting all their land and possessions to the king. Most complied, but if they refused they faced imprisonment, torture and possible execution, usually on false charges.

KEY EVENTS OF HENRY'S LIFE

~1536~
Dissolution of monasteries begins.

Pilgrimage of Grace begins.

~1537~
Robert Aske executed.

~1540~
Last monastery closes.

DRUNKEN MONKS

One criticism of the monks and nuns that could not be proved was that they spent their time drinking and having fun rather than worshipping God.

AFTER THE DISSOLUTION

Many of the richer monasteries were sold or rented out to the king's favourites, who might convert them into fine houses. Others, like Bayham Abbey, Sussex, were stripped of their riches and left to fall slowly into ruins.

RESTLESS SPIRIT

Like Anne Boleyn, her cousin,
also executed by Henry,
Catherine Howard's spirit
seems unable to rest. Her ghost
is said to haunt this gallery at
Hampton Court Palace.

THE QUEEN'S LAST JOURNEY

This is the last view Catherine
Howard would have seen before
her imprisonment, as she
approached the Traitor's Gate at
the Tower of London. Her only
crime was in having a lively,
loving nature, for
which she paid
with her life.

CATHERINE HOWARD

BORN
1521
❋

MARRIED
1540
❋

EXECUTED
1542

Catherine Howard became involved in the power struggles of Henry's court. Henry's marriage to Anne of Cleves had been a disaster and he soon began to look for a new bride. He was attracted to Anne's charming lady-in-waiting, Catherine Howard. Thomas Cromwell had strongly supported the king's marriage to Anne and his enemies were quick to encourage Henry to divorce her and marry Catherine as a way of getting rid of Cromwell. They married on 28 July 1540 just 16 days after Henry's divorce from Anne of Cleves.

FLIRTATIOUS NATURE

Catherine Howard was the niece of the Duke of Norfolk. She became lady-in-waiting to Anne of Cleves at just 19. She was high-spirited and great fun, which attracted the interest of the king.

KEY EVENTS OF HENRY'S LIFE

~1540~
Henry marries Catherine Howard.

Thomas Cromwell executed.

~1542~
Catherine Howard executed.

UNSEEMLY BEHAVIOUR

Catherine was accused of 'conduct unbecoming a queen' by Archbishop Cranmer. She was tried and found guilty, and later beheaded on 13 February 1542.

KATHERINE PARR

BORN
1512

MARRIED
1543

DIED
1548

Katherine Parr was the daughter of a minor noble, Sir Thomas Parr, who had risen through the ranks of Henry's court to become Controller of the Royal Household. Very little is known about Katherine's early life. Aged 31 when she married Henry on 12 July 1543, she was already twice widowed. Well educated, she brought a sense of calm to the royal court. Henry was by now suffering from many illnesses and Katherine nursed him in his final years. She supervised Edward's education and helped bring Mary and Elizabeth closer to Henry again.

PRESENT FROM AN EMPEROR

This grotesque parade helmet was given to Henry by the Emperor Maximilian I in about 1514. By the time he married Katherine Parr his face had become so bloated the helmet no longer fitted.

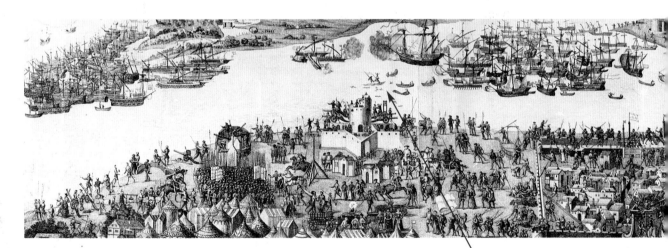

INSPECTING THE FLEET

Henry visited Portsmouth in July 1545 to inspect his navy in Southampton Water. He watched, ashamed, as the *Mary Rose* sank before his eyes.

This is where the *Mary Rose* sank, marked in the picture by floating bodies.

28

THE *MARY ROSE*

Henry's flagship, the *Mary Rose* (built in 1509), sank in the Solent on 19 July 1545. It was the first ship to be fitted with broadside-firing guns.

THE KING'S GREAT BED

Henry slept alone in the last years of his life in a bed similar to this one. He had become so overweight that he had to be hoisted in and out of bed by ropes and pulleys.

RELICS OF THE PAST

This fine collection of pewter plates was recovered from the *Mary Rose*. The wreck, and many artefacts of everyday life from Tudor times, are now on display in Portsmouth Historic Dockyard.

THE QUEEN LIVES!

Katherine Parr outlived Henry, although she was unable to give him any children. After the king's death she married Thomas Seymour, but died in 1548 after giving birth to a girl.

KEY EVENTS OF HENRY'S LIFE

~1543~
Henry marries Katherine Parr at Hampton Court Palace.

~1545~
Mary Rose sinks.

THE FADING YEARS

LAST WILL

In his will, dated 30 December 1546, Henry stated that Edward would succeed him as king. The next in line to the throne was Mary and, after her, Elizabeth.

*T*he sad, lonely figure that Henry had become by 1547 was very different from the strong, athletic youth who came to the throne 38 years before. Henry had always suffered from headaches, which caused him to become very angry. He also suffered from smallpox and malaria. He had varicose veins and ulcers on both legs. He developed gangrene, and smelled of rotting flesh in his final years. When Henry died on 28 January 1547, few people were sorry that his reign had come to an end.

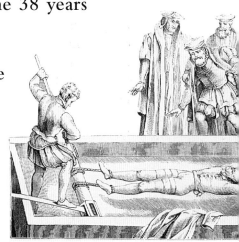

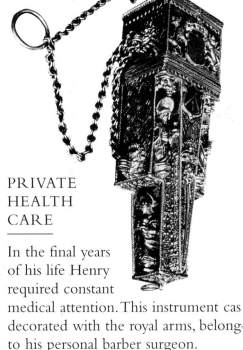

POWER STRUGGLE

John Dudley, Duke of Northumberland, one of the Council of Regency appointed by Henry to govern when Edward was too young. He later plotted to put Lady Jane Grey, his daughter-in-law, on the throne instead of Mary.

PRIVATE HEALTH CARE

In the final years of his life Henry required constant medical attention. This instrument cas decorated with the royal arms, belong to his personal barber surgeon.

SAFETY FIRST

The king became very worried with his personal safety in later life. He carried his own private lock when travelling, which he attached to his bed chamber door. Whilst staying at Allington Castle he had himself walled-in each night!

KEY EVENTS OF HENRY'S LIFE

~1546~
Henry makes his last will.

~1547~
Henry VIII dies.

REIGN OF A TYRANT

Towards the end of his reign, Henry became more tyrannical - ruling unjustly and cruelly. He removed anyone who did not agree with him from office. Thousands were tortured or executed by his order.

A WEIGHT PROBLEM

By the end of his life Henry had become very fat and disfigured by illness. He had to be carried everywhere by servants and lifted up and down stairs with a hoist.

GLOSSARY

Annulled A way of declaring a marriage ended or not legal without needing to seek a divorce.

Barber surgeon Before doctors were common, it was barbers who performed most types of surgery and medical work.

Bloated Swollen.

Caesarean section An operation to deliver a baby by cutting through the mother's abdomen.

Complied Followed a set of instructions.

Dissolution Closing down.

Forfeit To lose or have something taken away as punishment.

Gangrene A serious infection caused by bacteria in a wound. It causes the skin to rot and can lead to death.

Grieved To be upset after someone has died.

Hoisted Lifted-up.

Pilgrimage A special journey to somewhere (usually a holy place), or for a specific reason.

Tyrannical Acting in a cruel or controlling manner.

Varicose veins A swelling of the veins, often in the legs of a patient.

We would like to thank: Tim Feeley, Graham Rich, Rosie Hankin, Tracey Pennington and Peter Done for their assistance. Picture research by Image Select.

ISBN 978 1 84898 079 2
This revised edition published in 2009 by *ticktock* Media Ltd.

Printed in China.
9 8 7 6 5 4 3 2 1

Copyright © *ticktock* Entertainment Ltd 2006.
First published in Great Britain as a *Snapping-Turtle guide* in 2006 by *ticktock* Media Ltd,
The Old Sawmill, 103 Goods Station Road, Tunbridge Wells, Kent, TN1 2DP, U.K.